OHIO COUNTY PUBLIC LIBRARY
WHEELING, WV 26003

P9-DDA-709

MWHO 2JUL '21 C2 S0
A 18 13P S00UT5JY

OHIO COUNTY PUBLIC LIBRARY
WHEELING, WV 26003

Animal Habitats

The Falcon over the Town

Text and photographs by
Mike Birkhead

Oxford Scientific Films

J
598.918
Birk
1988

AUG 22 1995

Gareth Stevens Publishing
Milwaukee

029245

Contents

Note: The use of a capital letter for a kestrel's name means that it is a *species* of kestrel (for example, American Kestrel). The use of a lower case, or small, letter means that it is a member of a larger *group* of birds.

The European Kestrel hunts from a wall in London with the Houses of Parliament in the background.

A drainpipe provides a suitable perch for a male European Kestrel.

The kestrel, a kind of falcon, and where it lives

Kestrels are hunting birds. They belong to the bird family known as falcons. The kestrel is not particularly large. It is slightly smaller than a crow, but it comes fully equipped with a sharp bill, fierce *talons*, and fantastic eyesight, all of which make it a dangerous *predator* of small birds and mammals. Most birds of *prey*, like the kestrel, are masters of the air, with magnificent aerial skills which enable them to out-maneuver smaller and less agile birds.

To bird watchers and naturalists, a hunting bird of prey in flight is an exciting sight. The kestrel, like a lion, is king of its own *habitat*. It, too, is at the head of a "food chain" living off smaller animals below it. The amazing thing is that you can watch the kestrel in action right in the center of town. You just have to keep your eyes open and know where to look. Kestrels now live in many of the world's largest cities, including New York, London, and Sydney. Thirteen different *species* of kestrel can be found all over the world, from America to Australia. They are on every one of the world's five continents, but two species in particular are very common, the Common or European Kestrel and the American Kestrel. The worldwide population of these two species is thought to exceed three million! Some kestrels live on islands, too, with a number of species living on isolated islands in the Pacific and the Indian Oceans. The Mauritius Kestrel, which comes from Mauritius, a tiny island off the east coast of Africa, is one of the rarest birds in the world. In fact, there are fewer than five breeding pairs left.

Kestrels can be found in many different habitats, ranging from lowland river valleys to mountains as high as 11,500 feet (3,500 m). No other birds of prey can cope with such a wide variety of conditions. They can live on park land, open plains, and along railway lines and highways, while some species thrive in the center of the busiest cities.

Kestrels have gotten used to living in cities and are just as much at home perching on an old lump of metal as they are perching on a cliff.

The kestrel in cities and towns

Not all species of kestrel feel at home in the middle of towns. In fact most kestrels, such as the Barred Kestrel of Madagascar and the Fox Kestrel of Africa, do not live close to people. But in Europe and North America, the kestrel has learned to live side by side with humans. The town kestrel may be the Common (or European) Kestrel or the American Kestrel. These two species are now common in large towns throughout Britain, Europe, and North America.

Town kestrels don't look any different from their country cousins. But they do behave differently. For instance, they don't become frightened and fly away when they see a human being. They do not hunt in the same way, eat the same food, or nest at exactly the same time of the year as country kestrels. A town habitat is very different from the countryside, and, accordingly, a kestrel needs to change or adapt its way of life to cope with these manmade conditions.

As more and more cities have been built, kestrels have shown how well they can adjust to living alongside humans in their "concrete jungle." The kestrel's ability to hover like a helicopter makes it ideal for life among the high-rise buildings of towns. Kestrels don't build large complicated nests. In towns they are happy to lay their eggs directly onto a windowsill. This resembles a cliff, which is where they might nest in the countryside. Next time you are out, look up, and you might be lucky enough to see a kestrel hovering over your head.

The American Kestrel is the smallest of all the kestrels.

A female European Kestrel uses its strong talons to perch on a tree.

The kestrel's body

The kestrel is a good-looking bird of prey with a long tail and reddish-brown *plumage*.   When perched, it sits in a very upright position with its long sharp claws or talons clearly visible.   These are the kestrel's main weapons and are used for catching prey, such as sparrows and small mammals.   There are no feathers on the bright yellow legs and feet.   Each foot has three toes pointing forward and one pointing backward.   Together, the toes are strong enough to grasp a small animal so tightly that it cannot escape.

The European Kestrel is about 1 foot 2 inches (32-35 cm) long with a wing span of about 2 feet 6 inches (70-80 cm).   The American Kestrel, which was mistakenly called a sparrow hawk by the early European colonists of North America, is a much smaller bird — about 8 inches (20 cm) long, with a wing span of about 1 foot 9 inches (50-60 cm).   The American Kestrel is the second smallest falcon.   Only the

The male European Kestrel has a much more colorful and attractive plumage than the female.

The striking plumage of the American Kestrel makes it easy to distinguish from any of the other kestrels.

Seychelles Kestrel is smaller. Female kestrels, like most birds of prey, are quite a bit larger than the males but less colorful. The males, especially of the American Kestrel, have more striking patterns on their heads. Older male European Kestrels have bluish-gray heads and tails and very striking patterns on their faces — a white throat and what is known as a black moustache. Female and young kestrels have a general chestnut-colored plumage with a more streaked appearance. With all this variation in plumage, you have to be a very sharp-eyed observer to figure out what kind of kestrel you are looking at.

Although the kestrel looks like a big bird, it actually weighs very little. The Common Kestrel is the heaviest, weighing between 5.5-11 oz (150-315 grams), while the American Kestrel is even smaller at around 3.5 oz (100 grams). All birds are very light in weight because they have hollow bones. This means they are light enough for take-off and flight. Like other birds, kestrels have bones that are light and virtually hollow inside.

A European Kestrel's feather caught on a branch — a good clue that kestrels live nearby.

The head of a male European Kestrel.

The kestrel's head

Kestrels, like all birds of prey, have very powerful and attractive heads. The two most obvious features are the beak and large round eyes. And behind the thick feathers of the head there are two efficient ears.

Kestrels have excellent eyesight. They can see a lot of detail and can judge distance well. The large, dark brown eyes are placed at the front of the head and point forward. The down-curved beak does not interfere with the eyes. This means that the kestrel can see ahead clearly without obstruction. Birds of prey like the kestrel are very dependent on their eyes for hunting and, of course, when flying at high speeds. The eyesight of most birds of prey is about three times better than that of human beings. This is why a kestrel can see a small mammal or a beetle in the grass when it is hovering 20-30 feet (6-9 m) above. The kestrel can almost certainly see color. It is active mostly in daytime, although it has occasionally been seen hunting at night.

Kestrels, like other birds, have a see-through fold of skin called the "nictitating membrane" that lies under the eyelids and is attached close to the beak. This membrane is thought to protect the *eye* and is closed across the *eye* when attacking or striking prey. It is also used for cleaning and moistening the eyes. It works like a windshield wiper.

The sharp bluish-gray beak (or bill) of the kestrel is hooked at the tip and is designed for tearing flesh; it sometimes assists in killing prey as well. A mouse or sparrow is usually gripped tightly by the talons, while the beak rips the flesh into little pieces so that it can be swallowed easily. A kestrel's bill does a job like that of our teeth (like other birds, kestrels have no teeth). The bill also does the delicate job of *preening* the feathers.

On the upper part of the beak there are two holes — the nostrils. Birds of prey like the kestrel do not have a very good sense of smell, and it is thought that they do not have a good sense of taste either. They have a small, thin tongue that probably does not have enough room on it for taste buds, although some birds are able to distinguish the four tastes — salt, sweet, bitter, and sour — just as you can.

The head of a female American Kestrel.

A European Kestrel flies by as London's red buses make slow progress.

Masters of the air

The kestrel is perfectly designed for flight, with long, pointed wings and a slim, streamlined body. All falcons are fast flyers. The Peregrine Falcon is probably the world's fastest flying bird, reaching speeds of well over 155 mph (250 kph) when *stooping* on its prey. By comparison, the slightly lighter Common Kestrel is capable of reaching speeds of over 62 mph (100 kph). But it is much slower flying in a straight line, when reaching speeds of only 20 mph (32 kph) — about the same speed as a swallow or starling.

The kestrel's body is covered with feathers. Those along the trailing edges of the wing and on the tail are specially strengthened and shaped to create lift. This enables the bird to get off the ground and fly! Feathers are surprisingly strong, as you will see if you collect one or two wing feathers and flap them about. It is interesting that people have never managed to invent anything quite like a feather.

A hovering kestrel always fans its tail.

Kestrels fly using very fast wing beats, interspersed with occasional short glides through the air. But there is no doubt that the kestrel's speciality is "hovering." In fact, an alternative name for all kestrels is "wind-hovers." Hovering is a characteristic shared with only a few other birds, including hummingbirds and ospreys. However, in order to hover, the kestrel needs a good wind into which it must point itself. With its wings beating rapidly and its tail fully fanned, the kestrel can stay almost motionless in mid-air for several minutes. This enables it to fly silently and undetected above small animals and insects, before pouncing on them.

Besides having hollow bones, which make them lighter, birds also have *air sacs* inside their bodies which help to buoy them up in the air, somewhat like air balloons. Sometimes kestrels will try to stay in the air for as long as possible without even flapping their wings—a method of flight known as "soaring." Birds soar particularly well in hot countries because the hot ground causes the air above it to rise. These invisible air currents push a flying bird higher and higher up into the sky, just as they do the pilot of a glider.

Amazingly, a hovering kestrel keeps its head absolutely still.

Regurgitated pellets are a sure sign that you have found a kestrel's "feeding post."

Food and feeding

Kestrels are meat-eaters, or carnivores. They are voracious and efficient predators, with a varied diet that includes small mammals, small birds like starlings and sparrows, insects, and occasionally lizards and snakes. What a kestrel actually eats depends much on what is available in its habitat. Countryside kestrels mostly eat small mammals and insects that are plentiful in the fields and meadows. Countryside kestrels will also feed on a wide variety of birds and on frogs, beetles, grasshoppers, and earthworms. Without any doubt the kestrel can take almost anything, as long as it is not too large; some have been seen taking dragonflies, fishes, and even crabs! Most food items are not eaten whole but are held firmly by the talons and picked at and torn to pieces by the razor-sharp bill before being swallowed.

A female European Kestrel rips up a dead sparrow.

Kestrels have their favorite "plucking" or "feeding posts."

By comparison, town kestrels catch and eat very few mammals (as there are hardly any in cities) but make up for it with small birds. In a special study in Manchester, England, scientists found that kestrels fed mostly on small birds like sparrows and pigeons, plus a few mammals such as rats and mice. In London, town kestrels are known to feed mostly on sparrows and starlings. Towns often attract thousands of starlings each winter, and during the early evening kestrels can be seen diving into these enormous flocks. The average kestrel needs to eat around 1.5 oz (40 grams) of food a day: either a couple of sparrows, or one starling, three shrews, five voles, or a great many beetles!

Kestrels, like all birds of prey, cough up pellets of undigested matter such as fur, scales, and bones. From such remains we can identify what animals a kestrel has been eating. Kestrels often leave piles of these pellets on the ground beneath their nests, feeding perches, or *roosting* places. If you are lucky enough to find some pellets, you can take them home, soak them in warm water, and then carefully take them to pieces to discover what's inside them. This could be the start of your own scientific investigation into the diet of your local kestrels.

This adult Black Redstart is just about to feed its two chicks.

The hunt

Kestrels are daytime predators. They hunt on their own, covering the same area day after day. A kestrel finds most of its food by hovering and scanning the ground below for prey. Once it has spotted prey it drops down in a number of descending swoops or glides. Then, when it is certain of capturing the prey, it drops to the ground to make its kill. Large animals will be eaten on the spot, but smaller kills may be taken to a favorite "plucking post" or "feeding perch." Smaller prey, like insects, can actually be eaten while the bird is flying.

Kestrels make the most of the available food in their habitat. They have even been known to steal food from other predators, like Barn Owls. However, kestrels do not have things entirely their own way, as larger falcons have been known to steal food from them. Kestrels will also scavenge food or *carrion* alongside a road or highway.

The two Black Redstart chicks await their parents.

A kestrel photographed at the very moment it strikes the Black Redstart chicks.

On more than one occasion they have been seen hunting by moonlight. Even though this is thought to be exceptional, it is well worth looking out for them on a clear moonlit night.

Kestrels often hunt by direct attack; if a small bird is resting on a ledge, the kestrel will dash straight in and seize the prey with its strong talons. This kind of attack may be made by a flying kestrel that just spots its unlucky victim as it flies past. But sometimes it will actually hunt by sitting patiently on a telephone pole waiting for its meal to come by! Town kestrels are amazingly bold and will often make their attack when they are very close to humans. If large numbers of small birds are fed regularly in a park, a predator like the kestrel will soon realize that it, too, has an easy meal waiting below. It will not be afraid to take the opportunity of swooping down and snatching a small bird.

The kestrel has caught one of the Black Redstart chicks.

Preparing to breed

Kestrels start their courtship several months before the main breeding season, which is in spring. From late winter onward, European Kestrels start to defend an area called their "breeding ground." Defending a *territory* is not always easy, and sometimes there are serious fights between rival territorial birds. The size of the territory defended can be as little as 30-41 sq yards (25-35 sq m). Sometimes two pairs of kestrels will nest side by side on one electric tower. Once a male has established a territory he will then try to attract a female with a number of aerial displays. During most of these displays, kestrels tend to be very noisy. The most common calls are described as "kee kee kee" and "kik kik kik." Once you have heard these loud, piercing calls, you will probably never forget them, as they are very distinctive.

This female European Kestrel was injured in a territorial battle.

During the breeding season kestrels perform wonderful displays in the air.

Both males and females are capable of breeding when they are only one year old. Kestrels are monogamous. This means that one male and one female pair up and stay together throughout the breeding season. It is not clear, however, whether they stay with each other from one year to the next.

During the first stages of courtship, both male and female take part in spectacular display flights. They circle and chase one another, sometimes at great heights. The male may then dive-bomb the female, only veering off at the last moment to avoid her. There seems to be little doubt that the male is showing off to the female, pointing out to her what a brave and strong bird he is. This makes a lot of sense, as it gives the female a chance to decide how suitable this male will be as her future mate. It is extremely important for her to choose a male who is a good hunter, as he will later have to provide all the food for her and her chicks, starting just before the eggs are laid. Sometimes as part of his courtship, the male will bring food to the female. She then begs for it, somewhat like a chick does to a parent bird when it is hungry. This behavior, called "courtship feeding," also shows the female how good a hunter he is. The food the male gives her is important for building up her strength before she starts to lay eggs.

A clutch of three European Kestrel eggs on a window ledge.

Egg-laying

The male kestrel seems to decide where to make the nest, and to attract the female to his chosen site, he performs more aerial displays. The nest is very simple, often only a few twigs. Sometimes the eggs are laid directly onto a window ledge. Kestrels will also nest in holes in trees or on power lines. They may take over an old crow's nest or even use nesting boxes. In towns, kestrels will make use of all sorts of places, from inside air conditioning shafts to drains and gutters.

Some town kestrels nest in tree holes.

A kestrel chick stretching its wings.

Urban kestrels start their breeding cycle almost one month ahead of their country cousins, and sometimes they lay more eggs. This is probably because food is more plentiful in towns and the weather is less harsh than in the open countryside. Each female usually lays between three and six eggs. One egg is laid every other day. The eggs are fairly broad, oval, and a dull whitish color speckled with dark red spots. The female *incubates* the eggs for around 28 days. During this time she relies on the male to bring her most of her food. The male may occasionally sit on the eggs during the daytime. Both the male and female kestrel have a special area on their breasts called a *"brood patch"* which has a very rich blood supply. It acts like a hot water bottle and presses close to the eggs as the parent sits on them.

During incubation, the chicks start to grow inside the eggs. After about four weeks they are ready to hatch. Inside the eggs, the small chicks start to break through their shells using a very sharp piece on the tip of their beaks called the "egg tooth." Not all the chicks hatch at the same time. The oldest chick may sometimes be five days older than the youngest. When the chicks have hatched, the parent birds carefully tidy up. They pick up the broken eggshells and drop them a short distance from the nest.

These three chicks look fairly cramped in their tree hole nest.

Growing up

When the chicks first hatch, they are fairly helpless and almost naked. They are also very noisy, and they become more so as they get older. Like many newly-born chicks, baby kestrels are blind, and their eyes do not open for one to five days. Although the male hunts for prey in the early days, he seldom brings it right to the nest. Instead, the female flies off some distance to get it from him. She plucks it, strips it of all its feathers, and then brings it back to the nest for the youngsters. The female then tears up all the food and feeds it carefully to her chicks. As far as possible, she divides the food equally between the hungry chicks.

If the parents cannot find enough food, it is normally the smallest and weakest chicks that die. The first chick to hatch is always the strongest. This can cause trouble in a kestrel's nest if food gets scarce. The youngsters often become aggressive to one another, and even toward their parents. The oldest and strongest chicks attack and often kill the youngest and weakest. This sounds cruel, but it does ensure that at least one or two chicks will survive to reach adulthood.

These kestrel chicks wait patiently for their next meal.

When the chicks are really small, the female normally broods them to keep them warm. Young chicks hatch with only a few white *downy* feathers, so they feel the cold badly. It takes several weeks for feathers to grow and to cover their bodies completely. As they grow, feathers, just like any other part of the body, need a good supply of blood. But once they have reached their full size, the blood supply is cut off. As the chicks get older, the adults spend less and less time brooding the little ones. The female also takes less care in feeding the chicks. After about 20 days, she will simply drop the food into the nest and let the chicks sort it out for themselves. At this stage, the chicks are very active and spend quite a bit of time stretching their wings in readiness for their first flight.

Male and female chicks develop at different speeds. Normally, it takes the larger females a couple of extra days before they are fully feathered and ready to leave the nest. Most young kestrels are ready to leave the nest when they are 27-32 days old. Once a young bird has grown its first true flight feathers, it is said to have *fledged*.

This kestrel nest was in the ventilation shaft of an office building.

The home life of kestrels

After the young kestrels leave the nest, they spend about one month in their parents' territory before they set off on a life of their own. During this time, the young tend to stick together and spend their time "playing." If one of the youngsters decides to chase after a crow, the others join in. If another decides to bathe in a puddle, the others will join it, too. This is definitely the time when they learn to hunt and catch food for themselves. Young kestrels dive onto trees and rip twigs from branches to practice their aerial skills. During this month the parents continue to bring food for the newly-fledged chicks. At this stage the chicks compete with each other and jealously guard any food they receive from their parents.

In Great Britain, most young kestrels do not move great distances once they have left their parents. However, it is known that certain British kestrels have migrated as far as Spain and Morocco. Whether kestrels do *migrate* seems to depend on how cold the winters get. Birds from further north, where the winters are colder, will migrate quite a long distance, and some European kestrels will winter in Africa, south of the Sahara, in countries such as Zambia and Malawi. In North America, at the end of the summer, there is a general migration from the north to the south. Occasionally, if the weather conditions are right, it is possible to see thousands of kestrels passing certain well-known migration points within a matter of a few days. Such areas are well-known in both North America and Europe and attract large numbers of bird watchers in the spring and autumn.

Town kestrels can be seen at almost any time of the year. One of the most exciting sights is a kestrel soaring around the sides of tall buildings as it plays on the wind currents created by the buildings.

Right: An American Kestrel shows off its beautiful markings as it soars above the earth. Some kestrels fly great distances during their annual migrations.

A fox cub in its urban surroundings.

Friends and neighbors

Kestrels are not very sociable birds and only seek the company of other kestrels. Being predators, they are avoided by most other animals, but kestrels do share the urban environment with a number of other wild animals, as well as with dogs, cats, and other pets. As the kestrel flies high over the town, it might spot a raccoon, or even a fox, rummaging through garbage.

An adult fox looking for something to eat on a piece of wasteland.

This Brown Rat is very much at home in an old can.

Among the city garbage that the raccoon might rummage through, you may well find a Brown, or Common, Rat. Rats are probably the most successful of all urban animals, and they thrive in the company of humans — or at least their garbage. The Brown Rat's closest relative is the Black, or Ship, Rat, and they tend to compete for the same food and places to live. In this battle it is the smaller Black Rat that loses out. However, both species have their own specialty, and the more agile Black Rat has managed to thrive in a few select areas of towns. The kestrel will eat either of these two species of rat.

The smaller Black Rat is not as common as it was 100 years ago.

Other aerial predators

Without doubt, the owl is the only other bird of prey that has succeeded in cities as well as the kestrel. The Tawny Owl is common in towns in most parts of Europe. The Tawny Owl is not found in North America. Here, however, the Common Screech Owl has adapted most thoroughly to urban life.

Somewhat like the kestrel, the urban Tawny Owl has had to change its diet. In the countryside, Tawny Owls eat mostly Wood Mice and Bank Voles, whereas in towns they feed mainly on birds, including house sparrows, pigeons, blackbirds, and starlings. The Tawny Owl is a *nocturnal* bird of prey, very different from the kestrel in a number of ways. The most striking difference is in the face. The owl has a large "facial disc" of feathers around the eyes, while the sensitive ears are hidden behind these feathered discs. Although their large eyes help them to see in the dark, most owls rely on sound as well as sight for detecting their prey.

Another predator in and around towns is the beautiful Short-eared Owl. Unlike the Tawny Owl, however, it is found all over northern Europe, Siberia, North America, and Alaska. It is slightly larger than the kestrel — about the same size as the Tawny Owl. But it has much longer wings and a smaller head, with short feathery "ear tufts" that stand up when the bird is startled. The Short-eared Owl also hunts by day and may compete with the kestrel for prey.

The Short-eared Owl is a daytime hunter that may hunt in the same areas as kestrels.

The Tawny Owl only hunts at night and has adapted well to life in towns.

One of the most powerful aerial predators to be found in towns throughout the world is not a bird of prey at all, but the black Carrion Crow. This large bird may even chase kestrels and can attack their nests and eat the eggs or young. Its success is due partly to its being very flexible about what it eats and partly to its being quick-witted and "intelligent." The "clever" crow seems well-suited to town life, where it makes its living in a "streetwise" way. Crows survive in towns on scraps and leftovers. They will also attack and eat small birds and nestlings, a habit which has not made them very popular.

A crow's nest with several youngsters in it. Kestrels sometimes nest in old crows' nests.

Living with people

Living close to people has been a mixed blessing for the kestrel since, in the past, it has been persecuted or sought after because of its hunting ability. For centuries, birds of prey like kestrels have been kept by humans for *falconry*. This art of breeding birds of prey and then training them for hunting has been practiced for centuries. Many different types of hunting birds are kept for falconry — now done only with a special license — and it is generally true that the kestrel is a beginner's bird. At a falconry display, the kestrel always puts on an exciting show, especially since it has that extra special trick — it can hover. The falconer will simply throw the kestrel in the air, and the bird will go straight into a hover. Beating its wings rapidly, the kestrel remains almost still for nearly a minute, waiting until the owner throws a food offering for it.

Throughout history birds of prey, including the kestrel, have been killed in the thousands, simply because they are such successful predators. In order to protect his own valuable game birds, such as pheasants and partridges, a gamekeeper would have been rewarded for killing as many birds of prey as possible. The worst time for kestrels in Europe has been during the last 150 years, reaching a peak between 1850 and 1900. On one Scottish estate alone more than 1,300 birds of prey were killed in a three-year period, and of these, 462 were kestrels! The situation in North America was never quite so bad, although persecution of birds of prey was rewarded with a number of special "bounty" schemes. Pennsylvania once had its own "Hawk and Owl" bounty law, by which a hunter was paid 50 cents for every dead bird brought in.

Eventually the deliberate practice of killing large numbers of birds of prey died out, but something almost as bad took its place. From about 1950, large quantities of *pesticides* and other chemicals were used on farms to increase crop production and reduce diseases among both crops and farm animals. Unfortunately, these chemicals had a disastrous effect on many other animals, especially predators like kestrels. Having contaminated the prey (small birds and mammals which had eaten sprayed grain), the chemicals then got into the blood of the larger birds that ate the prey. One of the most serious effects of these chemicals was that the infected females would lay eggs with very thin shells. Then, when the female sat on the eggs to incubate them, they broke. Kestrels were quite lucky, since their population numbers were not as badly affected by the pesticides as other birds of prey like sparrow hawks and peregrine falcons. Most of these chemicals are now banned in Britain and North America, and the number of birds of prey has been increasing steadily over the last 10 years.

Kestrels, like this European one, are often used for falconry.

Life in the town

There is little doubt that kestrels seem quite at home living near people. They are not particularly shy, and you can often get very close to them. One of the best places to watch the "modern" urban kestrel is along a highway. The large grassy borders provide cover for small mammals, like voles and shrews, that the kestrel likes to eat. The kestrel's method of hunting is perfect for living along a highway. By hovering, the kestrels do not have to risk swooping in front of cars or trucks as they speed along the highways, so very few seem to get run over by traffic. Because the kestrel is a predator, it feeds on smaller animals that in turn eat even smaller animals or plants. Because it is at the top of its food chain, the kestrel is rarely eaten or attacked by other animals. Its only enemies are humans.

Food chain

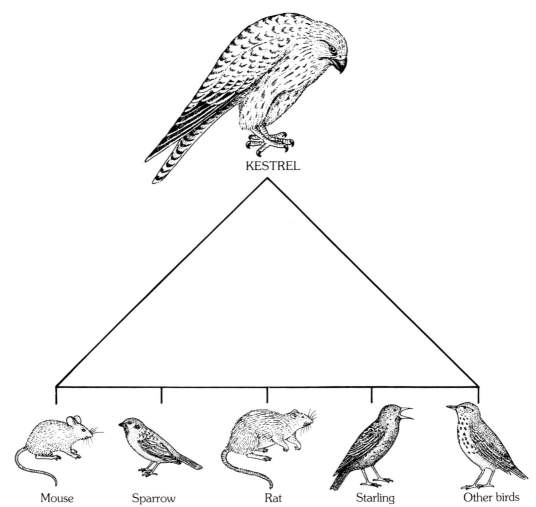

KESTREL

| Mouse | Sparrow | Rat | Starling | Other birds |

Keep a good look out for kestrels and you may see one like this hovering in front of Tower Bridge in London.

Towns and cities also offer kestrels an unusual variety of places to nest. Town-living kestrels love to nest on such manmade structures as tall buildings, churches, or cranes. Once a kestrel gets high up on a windowsill, there is very little to disturb it. All the different species of kestrel seem to be at home nesting on manmade structures, whether they be in Madagascar, Quebec, or Australia. Indeed, the German name for the kestrel is "tower falcon," and there are known to be over 60 pairs of kestrel in the city of Munich, most of them on buildings. In London and its surrounding suburbs, there are well over 150 breeding pairs of kestrel; and it is not impossible to see a kestrel flying majestically past Tower Bridge or Buckingham Palace. Kestrels have actually been introduced in some North American cities. You can actually follow the whole life cycle of this fascinating urban bird right in the heart of the city.

Glossary and Index

These new words about falcons appear in the text on the pages shown after each definition. Each new word first appears in the text in *italics*, just as it appears here.

Reading level analysis: SPACHE 3.7, FRY 6, FLESCH 77 (fairly easy), RAYGOR 5, FOG 6, SMOG 3

Library of Congress Cataloging-in-Publication Data   Birkhead, Mike. The falcon over the town. (Animal habitats) Includes index. Summary: Text and photographs depict kestrels feeding, breeding, and defending themselves in their natural habitats. 1. Kestrels—Juvenile literature. [1. Kestrels. 2. Falcons] I. Oxford Scientific Films. II. Title. III. Series.   QL696.F34B57   1988   598'.918   87-42615 ISBN 1-55532-329-4   ISBN 1-55532-304-9 (lib. bdg.)

North American edition first published in 1988 by Gareth Stevens, Inc., 7317 West Green Tree Road, Milwaukee, WI 53223, USA

Text copyright © 1988 by Oxford Scientific Films. All rights reserved. No part of this book may be reproduced in any form or by any means without permission in writing from Gareth Stevens, Inc.

Conceived, designed, and produced by Belitha Press Ltd., London. Printed in the United States of America.

Series Editor: Jennifer Coldrey. US Editor: Mark J. Sachner. Art Director: Treld Bicknell. Design: Naomi Games. Line Drawings: Lorna Turpin. Scientific Consultant: Gwynne Vevers.

The publishers wish to thank the following for permission to reproduce copyright material: **Mike Birkhead** for front cover, back cover, title page, pp. 2, 3, 4, 6 both, 7 below, 8, 10, 11 both, 12 both, 13, 14 both, 15 both, 16, 17, 18 both, 19, 20, 21 both, 24 both, 26, 27 both and 31; **Oxford Scientific Films Ltd.** for p. 5 (Wendy Neefus), p. 7 above (Leonard Lee Rue III), pp. 9, 23, and front cover (Patti Murray/Animals Animals), and p. 29 (D. G. Fox).

For their help and advice, the author would like to thank the following: Caroline Aitzetmuller; Ashley Smith and Rosie the Kestrel from the Hawk Conservancy near Andover; Andy Village and Ian Wyllie, David Quinn, Alastair MacEwen, and Jimmy Hull of the Oxford Museum. The publisher would like to thank the staff of the Havenwoods Forest Preserve, Wisconsin Department of Natural Resources, Milwaukee.

2 3 4 5 6 7 8 9 93 92 91 90 89